This book was devised and produced by
Multimedia Publications (UK) Ltd

Editor: Marilyn Inglis
Production: Arnon Orbach
Design: John Strange and Associates
Picture Research: Veneta Bullen

ISBN 0 8317 3938 X

First published in the United States of
America 1985 by Gallery Books, an imprint of
W. H. Smith Publishers Inc., 112 Madison
Avenue, New York, NY 10016

Typeset by Flowery Typesetters Ltd.
Originated by Imago
Printed in Italy by Sagdos, Milan

The
Great Lakes

Carole Chester

GALLERY BOOKS
An Imprint of W. H. Smith Publishers Inc.
112 Madison Avenue
New York City 10016

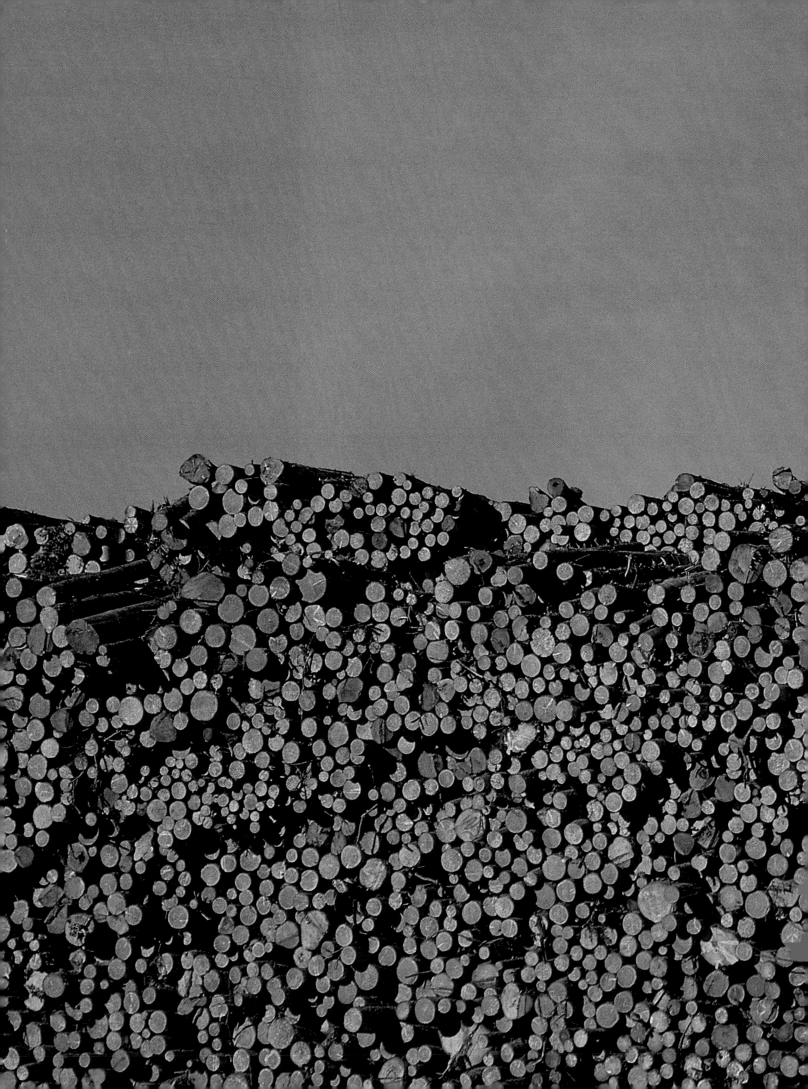

CONTENTS

CHAPTER 1

Water Land

Water for power. Water for transportation. Water for fun. America's Great Lakes land has seen the rise of manufacturing and industry and magnificent cities because of water. There are five major Great Lakes: Lake Michigan, Lake Superior, Lake Huron, Lake Erie and Lake Ontario, and there is one minor one: Lake St Clair. Some have international boundaries with Canada. Some are bounded by several states. Each is a marvel in itself; each has watery channels and offshoots.

The Great Lakes states are considered America's Midwest: Minnesota, Wisconsin, Illinois, Indiana, Ohio, and the greatest of all, Michigan. Together, they comprise the agricultural and industrial heartland of America. First there were Indians and much of the region is still rich in Indian lore and legend, especially in the north. They fished, mined, traded and settled in camps destined to become villages, towns and cities. They named rivers and areas of wilderness. They inspired latter-day writers to write stories about great Indian chiefs and beautiful princesses.

However, the roots of the Great Lakes land, in terms of growth and expansion, are mostly French, thanks to the popularity of fur. Many of today's large cities and ports were first fur trading posts used by French trappers, for whom the lakes provided the necessary waterways for shipping furs out.

Once explorers had penetrated the area in the seventeenth century, the trappers quickly followed, more than eager to barter with the Indians, followed in turn by soldiers to guard the strategic points of trade. In France at the time it was fashionable to wear beaver fur, so the trappers around Montreal and Quebec could expect to earn princely sums for the pelts. Less ethical traders knew that, and quite often cargoes of skins were hijacked along the Great Lakes. It was to protect such goods that

La Salle window purchased for Museum by Louisa St Clair Chapter D.A.R.

DETROIT

Antoine de la Mothe Cadillac came to what is now Detroit, little knowing that one day a car would be named after him. He picked the strait between Lake St Clair and Lake Erie for Fort Ponchartrain d'Etroit. It was French explorers Marquette and Joliet who provided the first record of the Chicago area and the black fur trader Jean Baptiste du Sable who was the first real settler. La Salle was the French pioneer who first wandered into the Ohio area, and again it was fur traders who discovered Minnesota.

Though the French teamed up with the Indians to fight against the British, they lost; it was only when the latter were forced to retreat to Canada as the colonies rebelled that soon all the Great Lakes states of the Midwest became part of the Union.

Vast forests were an asset. Timber became big business in many parts and logging and lumber camps were set up. Wood built ships and the lakes transported it. Wood was sent to pulp and paper mills, particularly in Wisconsin. Mining was another industry, and lakeshore ports were the obvious outlets for shipments of iron and copper. Then there was grain, cultivated in the interior and shipped out through clearing houses like Chicago. Steel arrived on the scene and with it, more and more related industries.

They call Michigan the 'Great Lake State', perhaps because it has access to four of those major expanses of water – 32 000 miles of shoreline and, in fact, thousands of lakes and streams within its perimeters. The St Lawrence Seaway turned such places as Bay City, Alpena and Cheboygan into international ports, and the automobile industry helped make Detroit an industrial metropolis. Its proximity to Canada has aided trading and, with two peninsulas, the easiest lake access of all.

The state industries manufacture innumerable motor vehicles and their components, boats, engines, refrigerators and office equipment. For outdoor adventure, Michigan is a playground par excellence. There are mountains and ski resorts; superb fishing and boating possibilities; state parks and the Isle Royale National Park; islands and beaches.

Right A verdant coastline shows some of the natural beauty of Mackinac Island in waters off Michigan's Upper Peninsula.

Left Bustling though the Great Lakes area is, there is still time to stand and watch the world go by.

Below A picturesque and tranquil part of Ontario – Picton, captured in the late afternoon sunlight.

Right Enjoying an ice cream at one of the best places for youngsters, Ontario Place, a waterfront complex with lots of live entertainment and amusements.

Below Fruit picking is enviable work if you have the chance to sample the goods as you gather. In Wisconsin cherries and cranberries are made into wine.

Michigan may call itself the Great Lake State, but Minnesota is known as the 'Land of Ten Thousand Lakes'. Actually, there are more, plus streams and rivers besides, some of which flow into the Great Lakes and thus to the Atlantic. There are still Indians in Minnesota, paddling canoes to gather wild rice, but most of the population is European in origin, as is the case throughout the Midwest. In the 1800s immigrants – especially Scandinavians – came in the hundreds, fleeing famine or persecution, seeking money, work and a new life. The Swedes came to settle the farms; the Norwegians, the northern forests; and the Danes to boost the dairy industry. Minnesota is often considered a 'transplanted Scandinavia'.

Lake resorts, the Chippewa National Forest, national wildlife resorts and a great wilderness area for canoeists are all to be found in Minnesota. State parks, forts and Indian reservations are constant reminders of its past.

Wisconsin is referred to as 'America's Dairyland'. Much of its rolling farmland, studded with silver silos, produces first-rate butter and cheese. The Danes who didn't settle in Minnesota turned their hand to dairy farming here, joined by Swiss, German and Polish settlers. The Midwest was so full of German immigrants that in the latter half of the nineteenth century Milwaukee was nicknamed 'German Athens'.

The dairy industry superseded Wisconsin's lead and zinc mining which had lured Cornish miners in the early nineteenth century, but the lumber business, largely built up by the Scandinavians, is still valuable in this state of pulp and paper mills. Cheap water transport, abundant water power and its important port of Milwaukee all contribute to making Wisconsin an industrial giant.

The Ice Age glaciers left Wisconsin with some 8000 inland lakes, particularly in the north of the state in forested areas where the hunting and fishing are first class. Not surprisingly, Wisconsin has 49 state parks, 9 state and 2 national forests, all designated for recreation.

Bounded on the north by Wisconsin and Lake Michigan is the important food producing state of Illinois, popularly known as the 'Prairie State'. Its major city of Chicago, situated on Lake Michigan, is the center of rail, air and water communications in the Midwest.

In its backwoods in the 1800s, when it was still part of 'the last frontier', a young attorney was growing up – Abraham Lincoln, who was to give support for the

Left The Detroit Tigers take a break from an inning of pro baseball. Other sports teams to look out for are the Lions (football); Pistons (basketball) and Red Wings (ice hockey).

Below Milwaukee on parade shows off the American flag but there are a number of ethnic pockets in this city. Strongest of all are the Germans who have given it its beer and bratwurst image.

Right Not all the boats on the Great Lakes are bound for the foreign ports. Pleasure boats take advantage too.

Below Shipping has always been the Great Lakes' strength. Between the five of them, their rivers, tributaries and canals, produce can make its way out to the Atlantic.

Top right Canada is synonymous with maple syrup. Pictured here are tin pails strung up to wait for the gradual collection of maple sap that will eventually become the sweet accompaniment to waffles.

Bottom right This old cannon is to be found at Fort Niagara, near Youngstown.

development of the railroads, canal and waterway projects and who was ultimately to become the nation's president. Lincoln memorabilia is scattered in museums throughout the state, and his name is associated with many of the state parks. There are a hundred of them, in addition to national forests and conservation areas which comprise 400 000 acres of land, almost half of which is occupied by the Shawnee National Forest.

CHAPTER 2

Lake Michigan

The Indians once used the place where Chicago now stands as the place to carry their goods and boats from the lake to the rivers that would eventually lead them to the Mississippi River. French explorers and traders used the shore front to beach their canoes, and the first permanent settlement established Chicago as a fur trading center – because of its position on the lake. Without it, the cargoes of pelts from Canada would not have reaped their trappers such rich rewards.

Only after the Battle of Fallen Timbers in 1794, when the US took over land at the mouth of the Chicago River, did the settlement grow into a prosperous lake port, though it was the opening of the St Lawrence Seaway that changed the city from being a lake port to a sea port with access for international trade.

One of the biggest growth factors for Chicago was the arrival of the railroad. And how did it arrive? By water. The city's first locomotive, a wood burner called the Pioneer, arrived on the deck of a sailing ship in 1848. By the end of the century, Chicago was the hub of a gigantic railway network. In 1900, too, the flow of the Chicago River was reversed to save Lake Michigan from industrial pollution.

The Indians gave Chicago its original name, and they called Milwaukee 'Good Lands'. In winter high waves lash the shoreline of Lake Michigan and its ice capped beaches are wreathed in snow. Though French fur trappers and missionaries visited this area in the seventeenth century, Milwaukee wasn't settled until 1800 and didn't begin to develop until the 1830s. What really gave it glory was its fine harbor on Lake Michigan, which was to prove it could accommodate the largest ships that used the Great Lakes and the St Lawrence Seaway after it was opened in 1959.

Sailing ships brought the immigrants to Chicago and Milwaukee during the nineteenth century. The Irish came in droves, fleeing the potato famine. The Germans arrived en masse following the unsuccessful 1848 revolution. And then the Poles. Many of these people were illiterate, and often waves of immigrants caused dissension and social problems because of their lack of work skills.

The nineteenth century was an interesting one in terms of industrial expansion when steel took over from timber. Chicago had already become the nation's largest rail center by 1856, and the rail network made it simpler to distribute corn and wheat from the Midwest prairies forming the basis of the city's economy. The first steel rail in the US was 'rolled' in Chicago in 1865; and after the city's Great Fire of 1871, which destroyed so many wooden buildings, the construction industry began to think steel. This was how the city's architectural splendor, still so evident today, blossomed.

The railroads brought livestock to the stockyards and meat-packing plants and then carried away the prepared meat to its destination. Philip Armour and Gustavus Swift built up their meat-packing businesses, and Chicago became the meat packing capital of the world. By 1889 Milwaukee had brewing as its principal industry; even today, city residents claim that they drink more beer than anywhere else in America.

Left The Prairie State of Illinois is often called "America's Pantry". It is a key food-producing region whose farmers are no backwood boys. Seen here is some of the surplus corn.

Below Indiana is a major producer of steel – the city of Gary, for example, is home of US Steel Corporation's main plant. Pictured here are freights of steel being loaded up ready for export from Portage.

Bottom left Said to be the world's busiest, the Soo Locks separate Canada from America. They accommodate more waterborne freight than the Suez and Panama Canals put together and provide the only gateway for land traffic in 600 miles of water-located international boundary.

Bottom Wheat is one of the prime commodities produced and exported from the Great Lake states. Once loaded, it will depart for many a distant corner of the world.

Any city with a lake on its doorstep has resort appeal, though the water here is rather chilly for a leisurely swim, even in August. Chicago's most popular beach is Oak Street Beach, where it's fashionable to be seen but it's unfashionably crowded in good weather. The moment the weather gets warm in Milwaukee people head for the beaches, which are only five minutes away from the downtown area.

Both cities have lakefront drives which are also used by cyclists and joggers. Milwaukee's lakefront has been compared favorably with the Bay of Naples, and at least one guide book suggests it's the most beautiful in the US. Three of Chicago's major parks are on the lakefront: Grant Park, built on reclaimed land downtown; Jackson Park on the South Side; and Lincoln Park to the north of the city.

Lincoln is the largest, encompassing some 1000 acres and named of course for President Lincoln. As an 'exclusive area' to live, the park itself also attracts numerous visitors to its zoo and conservatory where there are changing floral exhibits. In summer, outdoor concerts and an annual Jazz Festival are held in Grant Park.

Of the two cities, Chicago is the more brash and bold. It ranks first in the US for manufacturing iron and steel, electrical equipment, food products and agricultural machinery. It is a very popular convention

Left Needless to say, the Lakes generate a healthy boating industry. Here, outboard motors are produced.

Right Since much of the Great Lakes region produce food on a large scale, it is not surprising that farm machinery is big business besides. In the past new ideas have made people famous, like McCormick who got rich on his "harvesters".

Bottom The state of Michigan is particularly linked to the automobile industry. Pictured here is a line of the industry's products.

city, the communications hub of the Midwest and a financial center second only to New York. It turns over something like $90 billion in wholesale trade and $22 billion in retail. Nuclear research and the electronics industry also 'came of age' in Chicago. The city is headquarters for the major mail order houses and is noted for its furniture, radio and TV manufacturing.

What could be bolder than America's tallest building – The Sears Tower? What could be busier than O'Hare Airport or bigger than the Chicago Board of Trade, the world's largest grain exchange? And its ports handle well over 82 million tons of freight each year. All in Chicago, the headquarters for many 'Fortune 500' companies and for numerous large banks.

From the visitor's point of view, this city is notable for its architecture, its shops and its jazz. The Old Water Tower was one of the very few structures to survive the 1871 fire, but it is not the only landmark. The impressive Wrigley Building and the neo-gothic Tribune Tower shouldn't be missed; nor should the elderly Manhattan Building, the Monadnock Building, the Marquette Building and The Rookery. The gleaming Standard Oil Building and John Hancock Center contribute to the skyline, while apartment blocks like Lake Point Tower and Marina City make their modern impact.

The architect Frank Lloyd Wright lived and worked in Chicago, pioneering low, prairie-style houses like Robie House. Originally he studied under Louis Sullivan, whose last major building (considered by many to be his masterpiece) is the city's Carson Pirie Scott department store.

Chicago's Magnificent Mile along Michigan Avenue is well named for its glamorous shops selling chic merchandise, especially in Water Tower Place. Its cultural side is equally impressive, with a famous Symphony Orchestra, the Lyric Opera Company; and superb museums and art galleries like The Art Institute, The Field Museum and the Science Museum.

Art comes right out in the open in this city in the form of modern sculpture and murals by artists like Picasso, Calder and Chagall. They're fun! And so are the Rush Street bars, the Old Town pubs and the city's jazz and blues clubs.

Industrial big city Milwaukee has small-town appeal. Well over 2000 factories produce engines, heavy industrial equipment, electrical and electronic equipment, missile and aircraft guidance systems and precision instruments. Its breweries – Schlitz, Miller's and Pabst – all welcome visitors. It's a leader in the field of graphic arts and boasts a thriving shipping industry.

Facing page, top No, it's not the seaside but Chicago's lakefront! In good weather, locals and visitors flock to the beaches that border Lake Michigan for a well-earned dip.

Facing page, bottom The skyline of Chicago shows it is a port as well as a major metropolis. It boasts one of the world's busiest airports, the tallest building and the biggest grain exchange. It always has been – and remains – a great trading post.

Left Chicago is a city of immigrants who came originally to flee European problems. Italians are one of the ethnic groups in the melting pot. South of The Loop on Taylor Street is the city's "Little Italy".

Below The big and the small of it. Or is it merely to show however busy a city like Chicago, there's always a natural side nearby.

Milwaukee is justly proud of its county zoological park (one of America's most famous) and its Performing Arts Center, the hub of cultural and fun events with three theaters for all types of entertainment. Its lakefront Art Center houses an outstanding collection and at Mitchell Park Conservatory three huge glass exhibition domes display examples of horticulture and floriculture from around the world.

The city's downtown is compact and tidy. Bratwurst comes before hot dogs, and wherever you go you'll see food piled on plates in old German tradition. There is an upright image of honesty even in political circles, and compared with other cities, Milwaukee boasts a pretty good after-dark safety record. Much of that lake shoreline, by the way, belongs to the local tax payers who take full advantage of their fishing rights — and catch anything from smelt to coho salmon.

Look at a map and you'll see that Lake Michigan is bounded by four states, including the tip of Indiana, where the city of Gary is situated. It was chosen in 1906 to be the site of the US Steel Corporation's main plant. They had to move a river and pull down sand dunes and do some draining — all to make way for the steel producing factories. The red-glowing cupolas, turning out millions of tons of steel each year, make a dramatic sight, especially when seen against a night sky.

Facing page, top A typical Wisconsin scene of rolling farmland studded with silver silos. This is "America's Dairyland", producing more milk and cheese than any other state.

Facing page, bottom There's an aura of security and well being about Wisconsin, probably due to its rich farmland and comfortable looking dwellings. It is indeed a pretty, prosperous and friendly state.

Left Wisconsin's rich soil enables it to produce many fine vegetables. In this case ripe juicy pumpkins wait to be gathered.

Below Though primarily known for its industrial cities and plants, Michigan proves its worth in the farming areas too, as you can see from this picture of its corn belt.

Facing page Michigan's Upper Peninsula is a particular haven for the sportsman and tourist seeking relaxation. There are plenty of leafy forests and glades in which to take a picnic and innumerable rivers and streams for fishing.

Left When the Indians and the first pioneers first explored the Great Lakes, there were of course no city ports to tie up at. Canoes were landed on windswept dunes like these, still existing today on the shores of the lakes.

Above The shoreline of Lake Michigan is as varied as one could hope for, from well manicured parks to rocky outlets like this one.

Right Wisconsin's Door County is a Midwest version of Cape Cod, the breezy peninsula between Green Bay and Lake Michigan. Many artisans like this couple have moved here to paint and sculpt.

Below At Mitchell Park Conservatory in Milwaukee, three huge glass exhibition domes display examples of horticulture and floriculture in permanent and changing displays from around the world.

Facing page Milwaukee residents claim they drink more beer than anyone else. Brewing has been a principal industry here since 1889. The city is home to four major breweries including this one, Pabst — all of which welcome visitors.

Right Handicrafts attract many visitors to Door County which has become a haven for artists. Here is one of them, a print maker at work.

Below Door County used to be the place for hayfever sufferers because of its breezy climate. Now, all vacationers are charmed by its modest inns and interesting gift shops.

Left A bountiful cherry harvest is washed prior to canning.

Below Cherry-picking time is celebrated in the outfits of these two kids!

CHAPTER 3

Lake Superior

The almost 32 000 square miles of Lake Superior are bounded by three US states and Ontario, Canada. One of the most strategic ports is Sault Ste Marie, half-Canadian, half-American, spanning both sides of the Soo Locks, the world's busiest. These Soo Canals accommodate more waterborne freight than the Suez and Panama Canals put together.

From an Indian settlement, it became a fur trading center and mission station. The North West Fur Traders built the first canal around the rapids and by the 1840s, the center had split into two commercial towns exploiting the lake's timber and mining resources. First came the saw mills, then once the river flow was controlled and an electric power supply developed, the paper mills, and in 1901 the first steel mill.

On the Michigan side of the Soo, there are two parks with observation towers where you can watch the ships as they bypass the unnavigable rapids of the St Mary's River connecting Lake Superior and Lake Huron. Visitors can take tours of the locks to see a typical Great Lakes ore carrier moored at one of the Soo's wharves.

If Sault Ste Marie's locks are of vital importance to shipping at the eastern end of Lake Superior, of equal importance are the docks at the western terminus of the Great Lakes; St Lawrence Seaway-Superior in tandem with Duluth. Superior may be over 2000 miles by ship away from Quebec where the famous Seaway begins, but its enormous docks rank among the country's largest, handling millions of tons of ore, grain and coal shipments. Duluth, with its 49 miles of docks, is the exit point for lumber from Minnesota's northeastern forests and for iron ore from its pit mines.

Duluth was named for the Sieur du Luth who claimed this territory for Louis XIV of

France in 1679 as an ideal fur trading harbor. That port in combination with Superior is second only to New York despite the fact that ice closes the Seaway for as many as 125 days in winter. But Duluth is protected by bluffs hundreds of feet high on which the Skyline Parkway was built. From the parkway there is a splendid view of the great harbors and the city of Duluth.

There is another interesting view from the unusual Aerial Lift Bridge which spans the entrance to the harbor and is raised to permit entry to ships. Harbor and lake cruises allow close-up inspection of the giant docks and grain elevators, large freighters and the rest of the waterfront.

To the north of Duluth, the North Shore Drive runs 150 miles along the Lake Superior shore to the Canadian border for what is considered one of America's most scenic drives. Also north of Duluth is the 'Arrowhead' area – a wilderness little changed from the days of early explorers. Where voyageurs traveled by canoe decades ago, today you can travel through the Superior National Forest's Boundary Waters Canoe Area. The prime jumping-off and outfitting point is Ely.

One of the best resorts along the North Shore Drive is Grand Marais at the eastern entrance to the Boundary Waters Canoe Area. Continuing along the rocky north shore, at the very eastern tip of Minnesota, is Grand Portage, where traders once transferred their goods from boats to canoes on arrival and then furs from canoes to boats on departure.

Twenty miles offshore, in the middle of Lake Superior, is the Isle Royale National Park, preserved in its original wilderness form, with no roads for cars but perfect for hardy campers. Few changes have taken place here since the French temporarily annexed it to Canada in 1669. Primitive trails meander through forests, and almost 50 species of fish are to be found in its lakes and streams for those who carry the required fishing license. Some ruins of old copper mines are reminders that the isle's rocky shores were worked for copper by the Indians thousands of years ago, and then again during the nineteenth century.

Right The National Lakeshore has plenty of surprises, whatever the season. Lone dunes, sun-kissed beaches and green-clad land all add to the splendor of Great Lakes country.

Left Scene of the National Lakeshore Park along Lake Michigan. The Great Lakes not only offer a transport route for industry but are full of scenic pleasures.

Below Part of Minnesota's Lake Superior shoreline. The state actually calls itself "Land of 10 000 Lakes" and offers a variety of watersports.

You can also reach Isle Royale from Houghton, Michigan, on the thumb of land sticking out into Superior. The area around Houghton was America's first mining capital and also the setting for the first great mineral strike. Geologists say that the copper-bearing formations here are the world's oldest rock strata.

On the Canadian shores of Lake Superior, the 'Lakehead' twin cities of Fort William and Port Arthur constitute Ontario's largest lake port and one of the most important in the country. For centuries, until the first white settlers arrived, Indians had encampments here. Fort William was named in 1804 for William McGillivray, governor of the North West Company and was a key fur-trading post. Beside the docks, the waterfront is lined with car manufacturing plants, oil refineries, warehouses, pulp and paper mills, grain elevators and flour mills. Port Arthur claims to be the largest Canadian dry dock on the Great Lakes.

Left Winter snows may put a nip in the air but they have also bestowed the areas surrounding the upper reaches of the Great Lakes with many ski resorts.

Above The availability of fur caused many a Great Lakes trading post to grow into a major city. These days there aren't Indian canoes skimming the lake waters but there are plenty of gift shops selling Indian crafts like this one on the shores of Lake Superior.

Below The forests of north Minnesota provided the nub of the lumber industry and the lakes, the way of transporting the logs. Many of the early Norwegian immigrants headed to this vicinity to work with timber.

Top left One of Lake Superior's most strategic sites is Sault Ste Marie, half Canadian, half American, spanning both sides of the Soo Locks. It split into two commercial sections in the 1840s to exploit the lake's timber and mining resources.

Below left Busy Duluth, Minnesota, was named for the Sieur du Luth who claimed the territory for Louis XIV in 1679. Its port is second only to New York in importance.

Right Opening the massive lock gates along the St Lawrence seaway requires close supervision.

Left Millions of tons of ore, grain and coal are shipped out from Duluth's 49 miles worth of docks. Duluth is also exit point for timber from Minnesota's north-eastern forests.

Below Harbor and lake cruises allow a closeup look at Duluth's giant docks and grain elevators. Here, grain is being loaded to be shipped out to the USSR.

Bottom Thanks to the Soo Locks, ships are able to transfer past the unnavigable rapids of the St Mary's River between Lake Superior and Lake Huron.

Lake Huron

Lake Huron laps at the eastern shore of Michigan's Lower Peninsula whose forests provided a brief lumber boom. The St Lawrence Seaway made Bay City, Alpena and other ports along the peninsula accessible to international trade. It was, though, the automobile industry which spurred Detroit's growth.

Detroit is situated on the narrow strait which runs between Lake St Clair and Lake Erie. Opposite Detroit is Windsor, Canada, and at the other end of the strait is Port Huron, opposite Sarnia. It was the Frenchman Antoine de la Mothe Cadillac who founded Fort Pontchartrain d'Etroit ('on the straits') in 1701 and the British who captured it in 1760 after the French and Indian War. Though they were defeated in the American Revolution, the British did not give up their control until 1796.

While shipping has always played a major part in the area's development, it was the automobile industry which became the mainstay in Detroit and it still is. Nevertheless the Detroit River carries the heaviest traffic of any waterway – almost twice the amount of the Panama Canal.

In 1896 that first horseless carriage hiccuped its way through Detroit streets. A local engineer by the name of Henry Ford took up the idea and started his own factory, in so doing rocketing the city's economy sky high. Now it's the home of the giants – Ford, Chrysler, General Motors – a city which produces 95 per cent of all cars made in the US.

Ford's birthplace was Dearborn; his success enabled him to found the Henry Ford Museum and Greenfield Village here in 1929 to ensure Americans should not forget their past. Three centuries of American history come to life in this unique indoor/outdoor complex. Outdoors, in Greenfield Village, visitors will find famous buildings transplanted: the laboratory where Thomas Edison first invented the incandescent light bulb; a courthouse where Abraham Lincoln once practiced law; the house where Noah Webster compiled his dictionary; and the cycle shop where Orville and Wilbur Wright built the components of that first plane. You can get around the complex by carriage, hay wagon, pony cart or Model T, while a paddle wheeler operates on the lagoon and

a steam locomotive chugs around the Village's perimeter.

Inside, artisans practice crafts that have been handed down from generation to generation. Factories, shops and mills illustrate Michigan's transition from an agricultural to an industrial economy. The museum itself houses collections which touch on all aspects of American life including, naturally, numerous vehicles.

The automobile industry has given

Detroit its ups and downs. When there was money, it was a 24-hour town, as during the Second World War. In the 1950s, the middle classes moved away from the crime ridden center, and only since the 70s has a revitalization program for the downtown area cleared the slums and made it a better place to live. The city fathers knew they had an industrial powerhouse, but they wanted an urban showcase as well.

Right Old Detroit seen backed by New Detroit in the shape of the Renaissance Center, a vast riverfront complex of hotel, shops and offices.

Below Detroit sits on the narrow strait between Lake St Clair and Lake Erie. French founder Antoine de la Mothe Cadillac was not to know in 1701 that he would one day have a car named for him.

The 'new' Detroit boasts a riverfront complex of offices, shops, convention facilities and a hotel – the Renaissance Center. A ten-acre sweep of waterfront space – Hart Plaza – lures office workers for brown bag lunches, ice skating in winter, and summertime festivals. The Joe Louis Arena is another symbol of Detroit's rebirth, while the Detroit Science Center is part of the Cultural Center. The Institute of Arts here has spent millions of dollars expanding its facilities and General Motors have spent a similar amount cleaning up the neighborhoods surrounding its historic headquarters. The city's main street, Woodward Avenue, is now a covered mall, and nearby Washington Boulevard has tempting sidewalk cafés. And a touch of charm is provided by imported Portuguese trolley cars that link the Ren Cen, Cobo Hall and Grand Circus Park.

Like its Great Lakes sister cities, Detroit has a racially-mixed population. A Mexican-American pocket in the southwest; a Middle Eastern conclave in Dearborn; Poles in Hamtramck, and Italians in the eastern suburbs. And a favorite place for an evening out is Greektown on Monroe, the street that was the heart of Detroit's original Greek immigrant community.

Several tours available in Detroit give an inside look at its past. Stroh's Brewery is as much an institution as Ford, founded in 1850 and one of the last family-owned breweries in America. It offers organized tours of its lab, brew house and packing plant on East Elizabeth. Tours of Ford's Fort Rouge production complex at the mouth of the Rouge River in Dearborn take you inside to see how the cars are made from scratch to final assembly. There are also tours of the General Motors Technical Center in Warren (northeast of town), where you can see how ideas are translated from designs on paper, into wood, then into clay models, and finally into prototype cars.

Top As Ford's birthplace, Dearborn has become a tourist attraction. Costumed artisans in Greenfield Village here demonstrate crafts like mattress-making.

Bottom One of the gents you'll come across in Greenfield Village, an indoor/outdoor complex designed to bring Americana to life for today's generation. He is a veteran volunteer fireman taking part in the annual Antique Fire Engine Muster.

Above Visitors feed the deer in the unique 1000-acre island park of Belle Isle, a recreational area reached via a bridge.

Left Getting around Greenfield Village can be done by all kinds of transport methods. A steam locomotive chugs around the perimeter, but other choices include Model T, paddle wheeler, pony cart and hay wagon.

No self-respecting Frenchman would pronounce street and place names as Detroiters do, but many names are indeed French. Livernois Street, Bois Blanc Island, Belle Isle. Bellile (as they pronounce it in Detroit) is a unique 1000 acre island park from whose eastern end the Detroit River begins to widen into Lake St Clair. The island was originally set aside by Cadillac for pasture land. Today it is reached via a bridge and is a recreational area. The models in its Dossin Great Lakes Museum show the evolution of shipping in the Great Lakes.

Detroit and its Canadian neighbor, Windsor, share a common history – both having been founded by the French in the 1700s – and these days a mere two-mile bridge or tunnel separates them. Both cities were involved in the War of 1812. In the 1800s, Windsor was used by the underground railway that took escaping slaves north; and during Prohibition days, boats carried bootlegged liquor from Canadian distilleries into Detroit. These days, Windsor shares the auto industry with Detroit by having GM, Chrysler and Ford plants, though on a smaller scale.

Like Detroit, it is an international gateway on the world's busiest waterway. The port's five-mile frontage greatly facilitates the importing of raw materials, and Windsor has a land advantage, too, for five great rail systems meet here.

Similarly, Sarnia is located at the outlet of Lake Huron on the Canadian side, but it is only a bridge, tunnel or ferry ride away from its American neighbor, Port Huron. As an important lake port, Sarnia's industries include an oil refinery, a synthetic rubber plant, salt works and a boat building yard.

There are white sandy shores along Huron and many resorts and centers for both summer and winter sports. Between Michigan's upper and lower peninsulas and the two lakes of Michigan and Huron are the Mackinac Straits. Mackinac Island was a strategic military stronghold during the fur trading days, with a fort to guard the Straits.

Right Copper Point, Michigan is one of the departure points for boats headed to Isle Royale National Park where no cars are allowed. Ideal for hardy campers.

Below Left White sandy shores fringe Lake Huron and in summer on go the swim suits and out come the boats.

Below Right Not the desert but a Great Lakes sand hill area they call Sleeping Bear Dunes.

Right Fort Mackinac was built in 1780 to command the straits overlooked by Mackinac Island. This strategic military stronghold was fought over by the British and French during the rich fur trade era.

Far right Now a summer resort island, Mackinac has many scenic features and quiet charm. It can be reached by ferry from St Ignace and Mackinaw City or by air from several places including Detroit.

Below Manitoulin Island lies in the Canadian waters of Lake Huron.

CHAPTER 5

Lake Erie

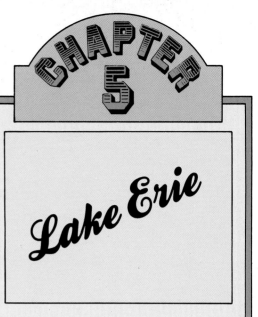

Lake Erie, almost 10 000 square miles of it, is encompassed by four American states plus part of Canada. At its eastern tip is Buffalo, an industrial city circled by 3000 acres of parkland. Like most of the Great Lakes, this region was first settled by the French, passed into English hands and later became an American military headquarters during the War of 1812. It began to prosper when the Erie Canal was completed, and within seven years the population had risen from 1500 to 10 000.

It became rich on flour, thanks to the introduction of a steam-powered grain elevator in 1843, which made it a major grain processor. Today, there are other diversified industries: iron mills and meat-packing plants that contribute to its industrial importance.

Pennsylvania also manages to edge in on the lake's eastern shore. The keystone of the original 13 colonies, Pennsylvania became a major commercial center while still a colony, because of its ports. Using those on the Ohio River and Lake Erie as well as those on its Atlantic seaboard, it was well able to trade with Europe and the colonies. Erie itself is Pennsylvania's great inland port, with one of the best harbors on the Great Lakes. Port facilities are protected by the Presque Isle Peninsula, extending 11 miles out into the lake.

The site was considered appropriate to be chosen for a French military fort in 1753, though it was later abandoned and subsequently taken over by the British in 1759. In turn, the British were driven out by the Indians in 1763 and Chief Pontiac ordered the fort destroyed. To prove its military worth, when the Americans came along, they built another fort in 1795. Most of Commodore Oliver H. Perry's ships were built here at Erie, from where he sailed to defeat the British in the War of 1812, securing Lake Erie for the US in 1813. He won his famous victory at Put-in-Bay near the lake's boundary line with Canada.

There is no need for greater shipping evidence than at this port. Perry's flagship, the USS *Niagara*, has its restoration at the foot of State Street. Not far away is the prow of the USS *Wolverine*, the first iron-hulled warship, built in Erie shipyards in 1843. The old Customs House dates from 1839, while under the Perry Memorial House and Dickson Tavern, used by Perry for headquarters, is a maze of secret passages where runaway slaves were hidden before the Civil War.

At Put-in-Bay, the Perry Victory and International Peace Memorial National Monument is one of the country's best, built 352 feet high to commemorate lasting peace between the US and Great Britain. It was Perry's victory over a British naval squadron during the Battle of Lake Erie which ended British control of the lake and made invasion of Canada possible. His message (famous in American text books): "We have met the enemy and they are ours."

The most important Ohio city on the shores of Lake Erie is Cleveland, stretching for 50 miles along the waterfront. Its location – where the lake and river Cuyahoga meet – provided a waterway necessary for the growth of heavy industries such as shipping, and steel and iron manufacturing and construction. Steady development began once the Ohio and Erie Canals were finished, and with the opening of the Great Lakes-St Lawrence Seaway, Cleveland became a major port.

Industry somewhat disturbed the original city layout designed by Moses Cleaveland (for whom the city was named) in 1796. But the city is notably progressive. As large factories sprang up in the nineteenth century, workers from around the world were welcomed, the reason Cleveland today is a mixture of nations and cultures. Most of the city's heavy industry and lumber yards are situated in the Cuyahoga River Valley.

Fortunes were made in Cleveland – by John D. Rockefeller in oil; Sam Mather and Mark Hanna in shipping; and the Van Sweringen brothers who created their wealthy empire from railroads and construction. The railroads, of course, aided city expansion, especially once they had reached St Mary Falls Canal, thereby linking Michigan and Canada. These days, as the

Right This old clapboard house stands abandoned on Kelley's Island, Lake Erie. Note the wooden skids underneath – evidence that the house is new to its present location.

Center Ohio offers varied terrain from its Appalachian Plateau to the east to the fertile Till Plains to the west.

Below The time's wrong but the place is right – Put-in-Bay, Ohio where Commodore Oliver Perry won his victory over the British in the War of 1812 to secure Lake Erie for the US.

steel mills continue to belch out their flames and barges still ply the river, Cleveland has become one of America's top corporate centers, headquarters for many large organizations.

Like Chicago, there are ethnic pockets. Buckeye Road, for example, once so full of Hungarians it was second only to Budapest, remains substantially Hungarian. On the east side is Little Italy and on the downtown fringe is Chinatown. Cleveland is no longer completely blue collar. Coventry Road in Cleveland Heights is a 'boutiquey' shopping area, and Beachwood Place a fashionable suburban mall. The city's orchestra is renowned and its Museum of Art nationally respected for its collections. Affluent businessmen live in Shaker Heights, a suburb where houses are large and streets wide and tree lined.

Public Square at the heart of downtown Cleveland is where all the main avenues converge. Statues here pay tribute to important residents. The Van Sweringen brothers may have lost their empire in the Wall Street Crash of 1929, but their Terminal Tower still stands in this square. The City Hall and other municipal buildings are located around The Mall; and Old Arcade, a

nineteenth century marketplace, is lined with book stores and galleries. There are several ways to see the water front, including a panoramic restaurant or a boat tour through the industrial valley.

Industry, perhaps surprisingly, manages to coexist with vacation spots along the Ohio shoreline. Sandusky, for instance, is not only a major coal shipping port but has wineries and resort hotels in its vicinity. Vermilion, too, is part of the Lake Erie Island region – stop in at the Great Lake Museum here. Lorain is an industrial port with a host of ethnic color.

One of the busiest fresh-water port facilities is at Toledo, yet another city serving the Great Lakes shipping lanes. It was here that the Erie and Kalamazoo Railroad began, the first railroad to be constructed west of the Allegheny Mountains. It was to Toledo that Edward Libbey brought the glass industry in 1888, but it was when Michael Owens became his partner that his industry grew. The latter invented a machine to form molten glass into bottles making the beginning of what is now a giant glass producing industry.

Much of Ohio's industry is inland. Youngstown, not that far from Cleveland, has been making steel since 1802, while Akron, directly south, has become the 'tire capital'. Akron's good fortune was once again due to the 1827 opening of the Ohio Canal, though it was after the Goodrich Factory was built in 1870 that Akron became synonymous with tires and other names popped up – General, Mohawk, Firestone and Goodyear. It is worth seeing Stan Hywet Hall here, the house built by Goodyear's founder, Frank Seiberling.

Top A Lake Ontario spectacle – Niagara Falls at the narrowest section between Canada and the US. Thirty million gallons of water cascade over the cliffs here every minute.

Right In summer several cruise boats offer sightseeing trips of Buffalo's harbor and the Niagara River.

Left Inside the pilot house of the ship, the *American Republic*.

Below Pier fishing in Lake Ontario is one of the ways to while away a few holiday hours.

Opposite Buffalo is not the place to be in winter unless one is involved with industry. This New York state town has a highly industrialized output.

Left Cleveland's steel mills at work. A major seaport on the shores of Lake Erie, the city's main streets were originally laid out by General Moses Cleaveland in 1796.

Below Super ore carrier photographed while under construction at the American Shipbuilding Company in Ohio.

Right The Old Arcade on Euclid Avenue is a nineteenth-century marketplace in the center of Cleveland, lined with stores and galleries.

Facing page The Boys in Blue help keep Buffalo on the up and up.

Above Photographer's idea of a cute name! Probably this Buffalo restaurant is not as bad as its name suggests.

Lake Ontario

It was the St Lawrence River, leading as it does to the Great Lakes, that attracted French explorers, adventurers and missionaries to travel deeper into the continent. Prior to the 1880s Canadians moving from east to west had to use the American routes south of the Great Lakes before turning north again through Minnesota to Manitoba. This was because the Canadian Shield was such an obstacle. In the fur trade days, however, that very same Shield area was the haunt of the much sought-after beaver, and those interlocking waterways on its rim gave ready-made canoe access southwards.

The St Lawrence leads quite naturally into Lake Ontario, one of the Great Lakes separating Canada from the US. Both countries were able to share the benefits of cheap transport on the waterways for such resources as iron ore. And indeed, today, 60 per cent of Canadians live in the St Lawrence lowlands. The area has had its share of turbulent history and battles for possession, notably around Montreal, Quebec and Toronto.

Toronto is the major lakefront metropolis. Originally, it was the French settlers who set up a trading post here and a fort to protect it in the mid-eighteenth century. By 1759, they had been driven out and like the rest of the then-French Canada, it had become a British possession by 1763. Upper-Canada's first governor chose the site (for its fine harbor) to be his provincial capital. These days, the city is an ocean port as well as a Great Lakes port, handling millions of tons of freight every year.

The town was called York, after King George II's son, the Duke of York, and only in 1834 was the old name of Toronto restored. It prospered but was dull and sedate — a place too good to be true where the sidewalks rolled up early. Only in the last 20 years as a result of an influx of immigrants has it taken on a glossier, sophisticated, more exciting image.

These days gold-tinted banks and finance centers reach for the sky, the lake is rimmed with waterfront developments, and old neighborhoods have been restored and revitalized. Overlooking it all stands the gleaming CN Tower, the world's highest free-standing structure, with a restaurant that revolves in a leisurely 360° turn.

Toronto has always utilized its geographical position, and nowadays does this for the visitor's advantage: Harbor Front with its markets and restaurants, its free entertainment and boats and Ontario Place, a giant pleasure playground for all age groups. Warehouses have been converted, marinas built and apartment blocks with waterside views erected. Ferries chug to the recreational island not far offshore and pleasure boats take to the Ontario waters in the summer.

Left Rochester's many parks and flowers make it a great place for a stroll. This young citizen steps barefooted into her mother's arms.

Right The reflecting glass of the Kodak Building gives Rochester a contemporary feel. Reflected in the glass are buildings from an earlier time.

Below The Eastman School of Music often gives free concerts and recitals in Rochester. The city's well-regarded Philharmonic Orchestra gives regular concerts in the Eastman Theater.

The most delightful quarter is Yorkville, where cafés spill onto the sidewalk or have shaded courtyards and where charming old houses have been converted into boutiques. A tiny Chinatown, a Greek district and singles bars along The Strand have added a colorful element, while Kensington Market sells everything from fresh food to old clothes. On Saturdays, the covered St Lawrence Market is good for food shopping.

Great shops are a Toronto magnet, from the glass-enclosed ones at Eaton Centre on Yonge Street to the 'Mink Mile' of luxury shops on Bloor. Hazelton Lanes is one of the most elegant malls, and Village By The Grange one of the most Bohemian.

Few people realize that Toronto is as fine a film and arts center as it is. The magnificent Roy Thomson Hall is home to the Toronto Symphony Orchestra and the city's Mendelssohn Choir. Best of the museums and galleries is the Art Gallery of Ontario whose Henry Moore Sculpture Centre contains the world's largest collection of his work. In the Ontario Science Centre there are more than eight hundred elaborate exhibits, many which may be operated by visitors.

Black Creek Pioneer Village shows village rural life a century ago: residents in period costume raise farm animals and demonstrate nineteenth century crafts, and the scarlet-clad Fort York guards bring history to life with battle drills and festive parades at the fort established in 1793.

Facing page, top. The Finger Lakes of New York State are a particularly beautiful area. In summer there are plentiful opportunities for swimming, boating and fishing.

Facing page, bottom There are always plenty of people eager to walk on the observation pier over the Niagara Falls.

Right A bit like the old days. This trapper has been hunting in Ontario where the fur trade which made the Great Lakes rich started.

Below The streams and lakes of the Great Lakes region are kept well stocked with fish, in this case trout.

One of Lake Ontario's splendors is Niagara Falls located at the narrowest section between Canada and the US. What a spectacle they must have made for Father Louis Hennepin, the first white man to record seeing them in 1678. Thirty million gallons of water pour every minute over the 200-foot drop of the three distinct Falls – the 182-foot-high, 1075-foot-wide American Falls; the 176-foot-high, 2100-foot-wide Canadian Horseshoe Falls and the Bridal Veil Falls. During the course of their history, the Falls have moved several miles upstream. For trade, they were an obstacle to reaching the other Great Lakes, though canal building helped overcome the problem.

The Niagara River carries the waters of four Great Lakes to Lake Ontario and Niagara has a power potential of about four million horsepower. Electrical production is controlled by agreements between the two countries so that each gets a fair share without spoiling the Falls' beauty.

Lake Ontario has given the cities on its US shores their industries. Rochester, for example, became known as 'Flour City' once the Erie Canal had been built, for the flour milled here was then easily shipped to large markets.

Facing page Perhaps to combat Toronto's cold winters, the Europeans like to add color to their homes. This community is not far from the city's Kensington Market.

Below Tobacco being collected.

Bottom Upstate New York looks very different from Manhattan. There are farms and vineyards, mountains and resorts.

Right Toronto is not only an international gateway by air but a communications center in other ways. This aerial shot shows it as a railway hub.

Below The gleaming CN Tower is the world's highest freestanding structure overlooking Lake Ontario on whose banks Toronto stands. It has a revolving restaurant and discotheque.

Left You may not find bargains along Toronto's 'Mink Mile' on Bloor Street or in the elegant Hazelton Lanes shopping mall, but there are some discount houses in town to help preserve the pocketbook.

Below One of the ways of getting around Toronto in summer is by sightseeing trolley. The most popular quarters like Yorkville, though, are best explored on foot.

Things to see around the Great Lakes

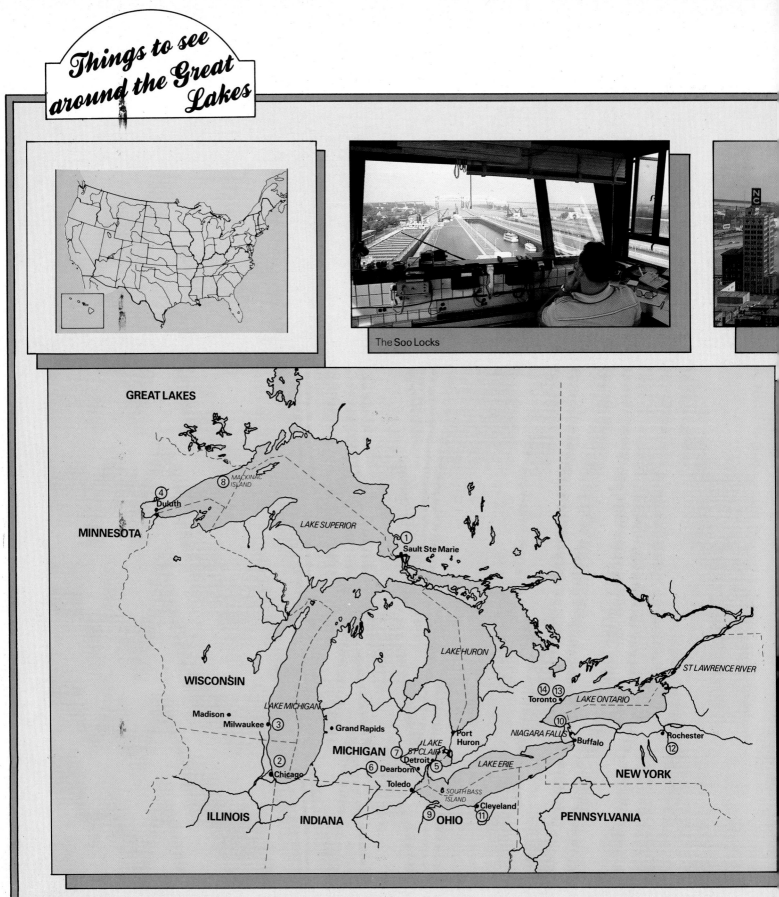

The Soo Locks

GREAT LAKES

MINNESOTA

④ Duluth

⑧ MACKINAC ISLAND

LAKE SUPERIOR

① Sault Ste Marie

WISCONSIN

LAKE HURON

ST LAWRENCE RIVER

LAKE MICHIGAN

Madison •

Milwaukee • ③

⑭ ⑬ Toronto • LAKE ONTARIO

• Grand Rapids

② Chicago

MICHIGAN ⑦ LAKE ST CLAIR

Port Huron

NIAGARA FALLS ⑩ Buffalo

• Rochester ⑫

⑥ Dearborn Detroit

⑤

LAKE ERIE

NEW YORK

Toledo

SOUTH BASS ISLAND

• Cleveland

ILLINOIS INDIANA

⑨ OHIO ⑪

PENNSYLVANIA

1 The **Soo Locks,** which separate America and Canada, accommodate more waterborne traffic than the Suez and Panama canals put together. Sault Ste Marie, spanning the Soo Locks, is half American and half Canadian and is one of the most strategically placed towns in the Great Lakes area.

2 Chicago's skyline is a magnificent panorama, encompassing the Sears Tower, the Old Water Tower, the Wrigley Building, the Tribune and Tower and the John Hancock Center, among many others.

3 Mitchell Park Conservatory in Milwaukee has three glass exhibition domes with examples of horticulture from all over the world on display.

4 The **harbor** at Duluth is second only to New York in terms of importance for cargo. There are 49 miles of docks which ship out millions of tons of ore, grain and steel, as well as timber from the forests of Minnesota.

5 The **Renaissance Center** in Detroit is a huge complex on the river where you will find hotels, shops, offices and convention facilities.

The harbor at Duluth

Chicago's skyline

Yorkville

The Renaissance Center

The CN Tower

Niagara Falls

6 **Dearborn,** the birthplace of Henry Ford, has become a tourist attraction and you will find many artisans demonstrating their varied crafts here. Ford founded the Greenfield Village, to which famous buildings have been transplanted; for example, Edison's laboratory, and a courthouse where Lincoln once practised law. You can travel round the complex by historic means of transportation, such as paddle wheeler, hay wagon or Model T.

7 **Belle Isle** is a 1000-acre island park, which can be reached from Detroit by bridge. It is famous for both its wildlife and its recreational facilities. Models in the Dossin Great Lakes Museum show the evolution of shipping on the Great Lakes.

8 **Mackinac Island** was originally a strategic military stronghold but is now a summer resort island. It has a special quiet charm all of its own.

9 **Put-in-Bay** in Ohio is an historic site from whence Commodore Oliver H. Perry sailed to defeat the British in the war of 1812, thus securing Lake Erie for the US. His flagship the USS *Niagara* is here, and the 352-foot-high Perry Victory and International Peace Memorial National Monument, built to commemorate lasting peace between the US and UK.

10 You must, of course, visit the **Niagara Falls.** At the narrowest section between Canada and the US, 30 million gallons of water a minute rush over the falls.

11 The **Old Arcade** in Cleveland is a nineteenth century marketplace, lined with book stores and galleries.

12 The **Eastman School of Music** in Rochester frequently gives free concerts and recitals. Added attractions of Rochester are its many parks and flowers, and the easy access to the Finger Lakes.

13 The **CN Tower** in Toronto is the world's highest freestanding structure, with a restaurant revolving in a 360° turn. From it you can admire the Toronto skyline and the lake beyond.

14 **Yorkville** in Toronto is a delightful place to stroll, or sit at a cafe on the sidewalk or in a shady courtyard. It includes Greek and Chinese districts and Kensington Market, where you can buy anything from fresh food to old clothes.

CREDITS LIST